On the Farm

Written by Kirsten Hall

Illustrated by John Steven Gurney

My First READER

children's press®

A Division of Scholastic Inc.
New York Toronto London Auckland Sydney
Mexico City New Delhi Hong Kong
Danbury, Connecticut

Library of Congress Cataloging-in-Publication Data

Hall, Kirsten.
  On the Farm/ written by Kirsten Hall ; illustrated by John Steven Gurney.
      p. cm. — (My first reader)
  Summary: A farmer spends her day gathering eggs, milking the cow, harvesting corn,
driving the plow, and feeding the horses.
    ISBN 0-516-24680-1 (lib. bdg.)   0-516-25115-5 (pbk.)
  [1. Farm life—Fiction. 2. Domestic animals—Fiction. 3. Stories in rhyme.] I. Gurney, John, ill. II. Title.
III. Series.
  PZ8.3.H146On 2004
  [E]—dc22   2004000242

6 7 8 9 10 R 13 12 11 10   62

Note to Parents and Teachers

Once a reader can recognize and identify the 41 words used to tell this story, he or she will be able to successfully read the entire book. These 41 words are repeated throughout the story, so that young readers will be able to recognize the words easily and understand their meaning.

The 41 words used in this book are:

all	food	mud	to
comes	gets	night	today
corn	goat	picks	up
cow	good	pig	wake
day	hay	plow	wakes
done	her	rolls	wants
drives	here	rooster	work
eats	horse	says	yawn
eggs	in	starts	
everyone	is	sun	
farmer	milks	the	

The farmer wakes up.

Here comes the sun.

Here comes the rooster.

"Wake up, everyone!"

The farmer gets the eggs.

13

The farmer milks the cow.

The farmer picks the corn.

The farmer drives the plow.

The pig rolls in the mud.

The goat wants food all day.

The farmer starts to yawn.

The horse eats all the hay.

The farmer says good night.

Her work is done today.

ABOUT THE AUTHOR

Kirsten Hall has lived most of her life in New York City, but spent many of her summer vacations on her family's farm in upstate New York. While she was still in high school, she published her first book for children, *Bunny, Bunny.* Since then, she has written and published more than sixty children's books. A former early education teacher, Kirsten currently works as a children's book editor.

ABOUT THE ILLUSTRATOR

John Steven Gurney grew up in southeast Pennsylvania and studied art at the Pratt Institute in Brooklyn, New York. He is the author and illustrator of *Dinosaur Train,* and the illustrator of more than 100 children's books, including all of the Bailey School Kids series. He currently lives with his wife and two children in Vermont.